SPECIAL OCCASION
Flowers

Text and floral designs: Jane Newdick, with additional
material by Gill Oakey; David Oakey; Wilma Rittershausen
Photography: Neil Sutherland
Editorial: Laura Potts
Design and typesetting: Lone Orpin
Original Design Concept: Stonecastle Graphics Ltd
Production: Ruth Arthur; Sally Connolly; Neil Randles;
Karen Staff; Jonathan Tickner; Matthew Dale
Production Director: Gerald Hughes

CLB 4666
This edition published in 1995 by Aura Books
© 1995 CLB Publishing, Godalming, Surrey
Printed and bound in Singapore
All rights reserved
ISBN 0-94779-331-3

SPECIAL OCCASION

Flowers

 **AURA BOOKS**

Getting Started

It is important to prepare the flowers and foliage used in the arrangements in this book carefully before use. If you are picking flowers from your garden, try to ensure that you pick them before they are fully opened and when it is cool, either in the morning or evening. Condition them by removing any unwanted lower leaves, cutting the stems on a slant and then leaving them in a bucket of water in a cool place for several hours. If the flowers have been bought from a florist it is likely that they will have already been conditioned, but to get the best results the stems should be re-cut and to left to stand in water for a couple of hours

Special care needs to be taken when conditioning some soft-stemmed plants. Poppies, poinsettias, euphorbia and some ferns, for example, have milky stems that need to be sealed before they are put in conditioning water. This can be done by singeing the end of the stem with a flame. Some very large flowers, like delphiniums, amaryllis and lupins, have hollow stems and these should be plugged with cotton wool, to help the plant take up water.

Woody stemmed flowers and foliage need a slightly different treatment. The base of the stems should be cut on a slant and, to enable the stems to take up water more easily, a little of the bark stripped away and the stem split, either by cutting a few slices upwards with sharp secateurs or a gardening knife, or by hammering the bottom few centimetres with a light mallet. The stems should then be left in water in a cool place for a few hours or overnight.

Time spent conditioning fresh flowers and foliage prior to arranging them will be amply repaid, the blooms staying fresher and retaining their colour for longer.

Orchid Bouquet

This magnificent bridal bouquet of tumbling dendrobiums uses a variety of foliage, including ivy, hosta and *Nephrolepis* fern, to offset the individual orchid blooms.

1 Insert a wire through the stem into the back of the flower. Then pass a silver wire through the back of the flower, winding it around the stem to hold it firmly in place.

2 Cover the flower stalk and wire with a thin twist of stem tape, starting from the back of the flower head.

3 Mount individual ivy leaves using a silver wire. Stitch from the reverse, then wind the silver wire around the leaf stalk and finish by covering with stem tape.

Left: Similar wiring and mounting techniques can be used to create a corsage with cymbidiums. Wire the flowers and foliage, then arrange the foliage around the two blooms, uniting the wires to form a 'stem'. Cut the wires to the required length and tape everything firmly.

4 Secure and tape single flowers with the ivy leaves to form individual units. Arrange five units into the basic design, fixing with silver wire. Add two central flowers and then the foliage. Tape the wires together.

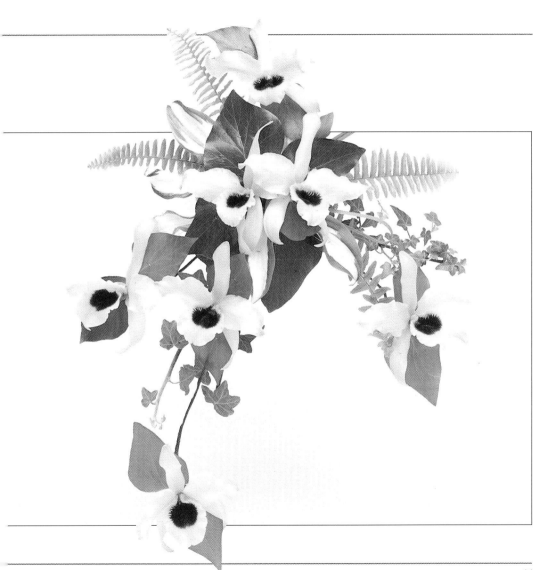

Classic Handsprays

This striking crescent-shaped handspray of orchids has been created in a foam bouquet holder. Using this type of holder allows you to feature flowers and foliage on their own stems.

1 Wet the foam bouquet holder. Insert sprigs of juniper into the foam, using them to outline the shape of the bouquet before adding any flowers.

2 Add stems of Cochlioda noezliana, pushing them deeply into the wet foam of the holder. Add more foliage and continue to build the bouquet into the crescent-shaped design.

3 Wire single flowers of Epidendrum radicans (p. 10/11) and insert into the foam. Insert two stems of Bifrenaria harrisoniae into the centre to develop a focal point.

Left: This classically simple bride's bouquet, made with speckled white lilies, cream and apricot roses and white bridal gladioli, can be made without wires unless the stems become too clumsy to make a neat handle.

Pretty Posies

This delightful posy,
composed of sweet peas,
fresh lavender and
Michaelmas
daisies and
complemented
by a delicate
paper collar,
makes a pretty
wedding
bouquet.

1 Make a posy up in the hand from a mixture of sweet peas, fresh lavender and Michaelmas daisies. Tie the stems with wire and trim the ends.

2 Take a coloured doily to make a collar for the posy. Fold it in half across the middle and then in half again. Cut out a central hole.

3 Cut the doily from the edge right into the centre. Pull the two cut edges towards each other, overlapping one over the other, to make a cone shape. Fix with double-sided tape.

Left: A single coral rose lies at the centre of this posy and is surrounded by sage leaves, starry London pride flowers, polygonum spikes, pink spray carnations and pelargonium flowers.

4 Now put the posy through the hole in the doily and pull the collar up around the flowers. Use tape if needed to fix the doily in place. Finish off with a ribbon bow.

Victorian-style Posy

This small posy, made in organised rings of different colours and types of flowers, is based on the type of posy a Victorian girl might have carried. Pretty, yet simple, it is a popular choice for bridesmaids.

1 Hold the central bud in one hand and begin to build up a ring of carnations around it using the other hand.

2 When this is complete, start a circle of alternate pink roses and carnations outside it, holding the bouquet steady in one hand all the time. Then tie it firmly with wire.

Left: A well-shaped, tightly closed rose bud and a piece of leather fern have been bound together with stem tape to make a traditional floral buttonhole. When binding the two together it is important to start at the top, twisting and squeezing as you work down.

3 Finish with a final ring of love-in-a-mist, then tie it once again, winding wire tightly round the stems just below the flower heads. Trim the stems to the same length. Tie with wire-edged ribbon to complete.

Bridesmaids' Baskets

The handles on a basket make it easy to carry and for this reason baskets are often a popular choice for very young bridesmaids. A very pretty miniature Victorian basket has been used in this arrangement.

1 *Choose a small, pretty basket with a sturdy handle and line it with moss all round the sides.*

2 *Put a small piece of damp floral foam in the middle of the basket. Start to put some short-stemmed roses throughout the foam.*

Left: Coral spray carnations, creamy yellow freesias and gypsophila – which has been used to fill and soften the spaces between the flowers – combine to make a more formal bridesmaid's basket.

3 *After putting about six roses in the basket fill the rest of the spaces with short cut stems of pale cream and pink sweet peas.*

Rustic Simplicity

A posy does not have to be made from expensive flowers to be effective. This delightful posy made from sweetly scented hyacinth is ideal for a spring wedding.

1 *Sort out all the different flowers into separate groups. This makes putting the posy together easier. Start to make the bunch in your hand mixing the different flowers.*

2 *Continue adding more flowers from the separate heaps aiming to make a tightly packed posy with the different colours well mixed together.*

Left: Though in itself simple, this bouquet of dahlia, pale green and white Euphorbia marginata, *deep blue delphinium, pink asters and small-flowered spray chrysanthemums has been transformed into something special by a bow made from two-tone wire-edged ribbon.*

3 *Start to add the foliage. Place the leaves around the posy pointing outwards to make a green collar to set off the flowers. Tie the bunch under the flowers.*

Romantic Circlets

The techniques used to create this romantic rose circlet can be used with other flowers, among them spray carnations, lily-of-the-valley, stephanotis and lilies. To achieve a more stunning effect suitable for a bride, larger, more lavish blooms should be used.

1 *Cut off each rosebud and push wire through the fattest part of the stem. Twist the wire once around the flower stem, and then push it down and together, making a stem.*

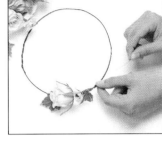

2 Cover the stem and the length of wire with stem tape. For the best results, work diagonally downwards, pulling the tape slightly to keep it taught.

3 With the underside of the leaf facing you, pierce each ivy leaf with wire, twist and bring down to make a stem. Taping is not necessary.

4 Begin the circlet only when all the roses and leaves are prepared. Attach them to the base using their lengths of wire, working round in one direction only. Alternate larger blooms with two or more miniature roses.

Right: Spray carnations, roses and gypsophila have been combined to make this bridesmaid's pretty circlet. To ensure a good fit, measure the child's head accurately and then add a little extra to the circumference to allow for the thickness of the wires that attach the flowers to the circlet.

Sophisticated Corsages

Making a lapel decoration is a very simple piece of floristry, as long as you choose varieties that do not wilt too quickly. This corsage, which combines a rose and freesias, makes an imaginative scented decoration that is perfect for a dressy suit.

1 *Choose a perfect bloom that is just at the point of opening from the bud stage and cut it away from the main stem, trimming away foliage and thorns.*

2 Select a short trail of variegated ivy and cut it slightly longer than the rose. Cut away the lower leaves, leaving the stem clear.

3 Take a freesia and put it against the rose, positioning it so that it extends slightly beyond the rose. Cut both the stems to the same length.

4 Arrange the rose, freesia and ivy in your hand, with the rose at the front. Bind the stems with stem tape, working down the stems and covering the cut stem ends.

Left: This romantic corsage is made from white miniature gladioli, pale pink roses, sweet peas and a sprig of honeysuckle. Attach it to a suit or dress with an extra-long, fine dressmaker's pin, securing it behind the fabric or putting it through a buttonhole and pinning securely under the lapel.

Floral Hat Trimmings

A floral decoration, like this circlet of cornflowers and carnations, can transform an ordinary straw hat into something extra special.

Below: Two old-fashioned roses, bound together with tape to make one stem, have been attached to a hat with wire to make a stylish decoration. A chiffon scarf around the base of the crown covers the rose stems.

1 Measure a circle of florist's wire to fit around the crown of the hat. Overlap the ends to give enough spare to twist the ends together.

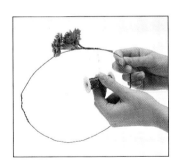

2 Start to wire alternate pink spray carnations and blue cornflowers around the circle working in one direction. Use a reel of fine wire for this.

3 Continue adding alternate flowers further round the circle, wrapping the wire two or three times round each stem to ensure that they are securely attached.

4 Finish wiring flowers and secure the end of the wire neatly. Place the circlet over the crown of the hat and fix in place with a few stitches or twist of wire.

Subtle Splendour

This elegant display of orchids is built
up around the stark, angular shapes
of the unripe seedpods of the common
peony-flowered garden poppy to make
a stylish arrangement to grace
the sitting room or hall of your
home for a special occasion.

1 Crumple a piece of plastic-coated wire mesh and push it firmly into the bowl. This will anchor the stems and ensure that they are immersed in water.

2 Position the poppy stems, using them to define the height and width of the arrangement. Insert sprigs of foliage to cover the wire mesh, working from the centre outwards.

3 Position the longest-stemmed orchids, pushing them through the foliage and into the wire mesh. These stems should echo the height and width of the poppy heads.

Below: In this lovely display, scarlet dahlias, red roses and yellow santolina flowers are offset with the soft green foliage of ballota and senecio.

4 Add shorter-stemmed orchids to the centre front of the arrangement. Fill in any gaps with foliage. Keep the arrangement topped up with water.

29

Altar Decoration

Roses, nerines and asters have been combined in this classic fan-shaped arrangement in pink and green, making a magnificent display suitable for a church. A pair of these arrangements would look good either side of the altar.

1 Soak a block of floral foam and put it in a waterproof container or on a plate. Put some stems of foliage in place to set the size and shape of the arrangement.

2 Add more stems of foliage of several different kinds aiming for a fan-shaped silhouette. Bring some shorter stems forward from the arrangement.

3 Now add stems of flowers starting at the back and filling in between the foliage. Put some blooms such as the pink roses facing forward and equally spaced.

4 Continue adding blooms such as nerines and asters amongst the arrangement to make a full effect. Make sure the flowers cover the foam near the base of the arrangement.

Colourful and Classic

In this formal arrangement, brilliant scarlet crocosmia, nasturtiums and yellow lilies have been combined with yellow clematis to give a spectacular explosion of late summer colour.

3 *Build up the arrangement with yellow lilies, nasturtiums and their leaves, and a few stems of fennel flowers. Then add some trails of clematis.*

1 *Put a block of damp floral foam into the vase. Cover it with crumpled wire netting, tucking the edges under the neck of the vase.*

2 *Start by putting a few large pieces of foliage and the stems of crocosmia in place to establish the overall size and shape of the finished arrangement.*

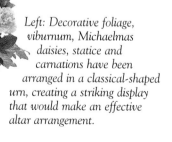

Left: Decorative foliage, viburnum, Michaelmas daisies, statice and carnations have been arranged in a classical-shaped urn, creating a striking display that would make an effective altar arrangement.

4 *Finally, put clematis flowers and a few of the fluffy seedheads throughout the arrangement. Fill any spaces with nasturtiums.*

Country Wedding

A long, narrow basket filled with pale mauve-blue scabious makes a striking, yet informal, display that would be ideal for a narrow windowsill of a country church.

1 Fill a long shallow basket with damp floral foam. Add sprigs of apple mint along the middle of the basket to set the size and outline.

2 Add white lace flower cut with short stems in a row across the basket. Then add lavatera and stokesia, facing them forward.

3 Finally, finish off by adding the scabious flowers throughout the arrangement. About twelve were used here.

Right: Here, an informal basket of flowers, containing roses, lilies, chrysanthemums, alstroemeria and gypsophila, has been used to decorate a stone font. For this arrangement, secure the flowers in wire mesh contained in a watertight container.

Decorative Pew End

Nothing is prettier than a church bedecked with fresh flowers. Pew ends, echoing the colour theme of the bride's and bridesmaids' bouquets, are an effective way to decorate a church for a wedding.

1 You will need a special plastic container. Cut damp floral foam to fit the base, push it into place, then snap the lid over it. It should lock itself tightly shut.

2 Hang the frame in a vertical position. Cover the foam with foliage, starting with long stems of ivy, then adding smaller pieces of variegated euonymus and green hellebore flowers to the centre.

3 Now put small sprigs of mauve statice and Michaelmas daisies in amongst the foliage background. Make sure the sides are covered too.

Right: This arrangement is most effective when seen from above and would be ideal for a low table at the entrance of a church. It uses short-stemmed flowers arranged in concentric circles in a circular piece of damp floral foam.

4 Split a bunch of apricot spray carnations up into single flower heads and put these evenly through the arrangement. Finish off with a ribbon bow and attach with a strong wire loop to the pew.

Reception Centrepieces

Michaelmas daisies, variegated periwinkle, freesias and *Ornithogolum arabicum* have been arranged in a tall-stemmed glass dish creating a magnificent table centrepiece suitable for a wedding reception or other special occasion.

1 *Cut a block of floral foam to the correct size, making sure that it is not too high. Soak the foam, then tape it firmly into place.*

2 *Cover the foam with stems of variegated periwinkle. Add small sprigs of Michaelmas daisy, making a rounded shape to the outline. Add a few Ornithogolum arabicum.*

Left: This sweet, pretty arrangement of pink roses, fragrant sweet peas, chrysanthemums and Michaelmas daisies in a long-stemmed glass candle holder is perfect for the celebration table at a christening party.

3 *Now put mauve freesias throughout the arrangement, spacing them evenly to make a balanced and symmetrical shape and keeping the outline smooth.*

Celebration Baskets

A wide, flat basket provides the perfect container for this arrangement of *Dendrobium* Bom and *Dendrobium* Big White. With flowers piled up and spilling gracefully out over the sides of the basket, the arrangement is a perfect centrepiece for a large celebration table.

1 Secure a piece of damp floral foam to a bowl with crossed lengths of tape. Attach the bowl to the basket with lengths of adhesive strip.

2 Insert foliage into the foam, using it to set the height and width of the arrangement. Try to make use of the natural curves of the stems.

3 Insert the longest flower stems into the sides of the foam. Then build up the arrangement, keeping within the confines of the handle and using the minimum amount of foliage.

Left: This spectacular display of pink and white hyacinths has also been created in a low-sided basket. Colourful and sweetly scented, the arrangement makes a perfect decoration for a buffet table.

Buffet Bonanza

Bring a touch of opulence to an evening buffet table with this spectacular pyramid of fruit. A few lily blooms, clusters of rose hips and pieces of trailing foliage transform the simple into the sublime.

1 Arrange a selection of different fruits onto a stemmed dish. Then tuck small clusters of rose hips or berries in amongst the polished fruits.

2 Now take four lily flower heads cut from a single stem and push them in amongst the fruit, facing them in different directions.

3 Finally, for a colour contrast, add a spray or two of foliage to set off the fruits and flowers.

Left: Combine glossy dark green leaves and brilliant orangey red alstromeria flower heads, to make a rich, vibrant display.

Marquee Magic

This delightful hanging ball adds a touch of sumptuous elegance to the interior of a wedding marquee. Covered in fresh flowers, the arrangement makes an unusual alternative to a traditional garland or swag.

1 *Push a stick right through the axis of a well-soaked, medium-sized floral foam ball. Leave it in place. Cut the stems of the flower heads very short and start to push them into the ball.*

Right: The basis of this magnificent pompom tree is a floral foam ball attached to a stick and secured in a ready-bought oasis-filled pot. Placed in a silver ice bucket, the arrangement, which includes lilies, orchids and gypsophila, makes an ideal decoration for a wedding reception.

2 *Continue adding large flower heads, turning the ball as you go. Fill any gaps in the foam with small bunches of waxflower.*

3 Attach a piece of string to the stick.
   Pull the stick clear of the ball. Leave
   extra string at the bottom of the ball
   and remove the stick.

4 Tie a small piece of twig to the
   string at the bottom of the ball, then
   pull the string back up. Finish by
   winding a little small-leaved ivy
   around the hanging string.

Sweet and Simple

Simplicity is often the key to success. This easy table arrangement in a blue-and-white china soup plate uses the plate's pretty border as an edging to the finished display.

Below: A cake decorated with fresh flower heads can look stunning. Here, a christening cake has been decorated with Michaelmas daisies and a tiny bunch of flowers, including lavender, forget-me-nots and chicory flower.

1 Cut a piece of foam to the right size, wet it and push it onto a pin holder. Position this in the centre of the plate.

2 Cut all the flowers short. Put the first rose in place in the centre. Arrange a ring of cornflowers around the central rose.

3 Add a ring of scabious flowers. Complete the arrangement with a ring of roses, placing them inside the rim of the dish. Top up the dish with water for the roses.

Birthday Celebration

Use different varieties
of miniature daffodils to
create a fresh-looking
spring display to
decorate the table
at a special
birthday
celebration.

1 Using a foam base makes wreath construction very quick and easy. Soak the ring thoroughly before starting to put small flowers and leaves in place.

2 Continue adding flowers, mixing the colours and varieties throughout the wreath and working round in one direction.

3 When you have covered right round to the start check that the inner edge is well covered. Fix a wire loop to the back for hanging the wreath.

Right: A very special birthday and a fitting cake to celebrate it with. Heads of delicate golden alstroemeria are simply laid all round the cake base and are easily removed when it comes to cutting it.

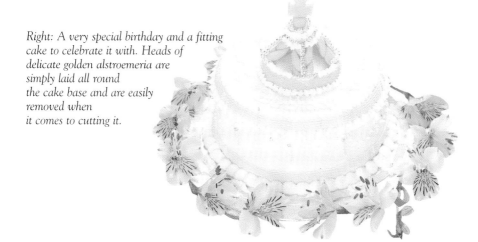

Bouquets for Giving

One of the most welcome gifts you can give to anyone is a posy of flowers. Here, lilac, sweet peas and statice have been combined with apricot roses to make a sweetly scented bunch.

1 If the roses are floribunda types, begin by separating them into single stems and clean off the thorns and leaves.

2 First hold one or two stems tightly in one hand and add another flower with the other hand. Do not worry if at this stage the stems are all different lengths.

3 Continue adding blooms, mixing the colours and varieties as much as possible and working round evenly. Hold the bunch as tightly as possible.

4 Cut the stems to the same length and secure the bouquet with a rubber band. Cover the rubber band with ribbon and tie an attractive bow.

Right: A thin gold cord wrapped around the stem and a ruffle of brightly coloured wire-edged ribbon have been used to transform a posy of ranunculus in shades of pink, peach and apricot into something extra special.

Presentation Posies

Nestling in a box amid tissue paper, a simple posy can make a sophisticated gift for a birthday or anniversary. Here, a pretty posy of violets has been offset with a collar of variegated ivy.

1 Collect the violet blooms together and make them into a small bunch in your hand keeping the flower heads all together at roughly the same level.

2 Add a collar of small variegated ivy leaves all around the violet posy. When you have completely surrounded the violets with leaves tie the stems together with wire.

Left: A pale blue tissue paper collar has been used to complement a loosely arranged posy of anemones. To make the collar cut a row of points along the long edge of three pieces of tissue paper, then wrap them around the posy just beneath the flower heads.

3 Finally, trim the stems of the violet posy neatly across at the bottom, leaving enough stem length for whatever purpose you have in mind.

Scented Extravaganza

Pink and white lilies, white amaryllis and red roses have been combined to make a dramatic bouquet that would make a memorable gift. To avoid any nasty stains remove the pollen-laden stamens of the lilies.

1 Prepare the roses and lilies, cutting off any lower leaves. Cut off the lower leaves of some Euphorbia marginata and gather together red roses, 'Stargazer' lilies and white amaryllis.

2 Start to make the bouquet in your hand. An amaryllis should be the basis with some euphorbia added to it. Next include a rose, then a lily and so on.

3 When the bouquet is full and complete tie wire around the stems just under the flowers and trim off the stems to a comfortable length. Cover the wire with a ribbon and tie into a floppy bow.

Left: This beautiful bunch of mixed flowers, featuring deep purple irises, pinks, sweet peas, alstroemeria and unusual, quilled- petal chrysanthemums, would be perfect to take to a dinner party as a gift.

Christmas Table

In this arrangement, red anemones have been combined with glossy evergreen foliage and variegated euonymus to create an eye-catching, seasonal display suitable for a festive table.

3 *Now put about eight to ten red anemones in amongst the foliage, spacing them out equally all around the ring.*

1 *Fill a ring dish or a metal ring mould with damp moss. Snip the variegated euonymus and Garrya elliptica into small manageable pieces.*

2 *Push the pieces of foliage firmly into the moss, alternating the variegated euonymus and Garrya elliptica around the dish.*

4 *Loop a length of ribbon several times and then secure it with stub wire. Push this down into the centre of the ring.*

Left: Sprigs of fir and velvety red anemones have been used to encircle a gold candle. A row of these would look lovely running the length of a dining table or at each place setting for a Christmas meal.

Christmas Party

Bring a festive touch to your home with
this attractive Christmas
decoration. Variegated
ivy, roses and
coloured baubles
have been
combined to
make a stylish
seasonal
arrangement.

1 Begin to make a small bunch in your hand of red roses and small gold baubles which have been fixed to lengths of wire.

2 Now start to add some trails of small-leaved variegated ivy around and amongst the roses. Continue to build up the bunch with more roses and baubles.

3 Finish the bunch with one or two much longer trails of ivy. Tie the stems of the bunch together high up under the flowers with wire.

Left: Tiny kumquat oranges spiked onto short lengths of wire add the colour to this dish of evergreen foliage and long, slim flower candles. Little spotted bows add a light-hearted touch. To create this arrangement, cut a block of floral foam to cover the dish and push leaves, candles and wires straight into it.

4 Finish off the bunch with a decoration of red raffia. Use several strands and wrap them a few times around the stems before tying them.

Acknowledgements

The publishers are grateful to the following for the provision of the flowers featured in this book.

Pepi Dillulo

Laurence Hobbs

Spriggs Florists, Petworth

Southdown Flowers, Yapton